Date: 8/6/12

BIG DOGS RULE

German Shepherd
Super Smart

by Natalie Lunis

Consultant: James C. Dascoli
President, Garden State German Shepherd Rescue

BEARPORT
PUBLISHING

New York, New York

Credits

Cover and Title Page, © Nikolai Tsvetkov/Shutterstock; TOC, © Eric Isselée/Shutterstock; 4, © Marc Lester/ Anchorage Daily News/MCT/Landov; 5, © Jody Garland/AFP/Getty Images; 6, © AP Photo/Mark Thiessen; 7, © AP Photo/Mark Thiessen; 8, © Mary Evans Picture Library; 9L, © Aurelia Ventura/LA Opinion/Newscom; 9R, © AP Photo/Stephen Chernin; 10, © F1 Online/SuperStock; 11L, © Mary Evans Picture Library/Everett Collection; 11R, From the book Der Deutsche Schäferhunde in Wort und Bild, 1932, Adolf Schulz archive; 12, © Popperfoto/ Getty Images; 13TR, © Hulton Archive/Getty Images; 13TL, © Everett Collection; 13B, © AP Photo; 14T, © Minden Pictures/SuperStock; 14B, © Dushenina/Shutterstock; 15L, © AP Photo/Journal Newspaper/Ron Agnir; 15R, © Petra Wegner/Alamy; 16, © Animals Animals/SuperStock; 17TL, © helza/Shutterstock; 17TR, © Jeannie Harrison/Close Encounters of the Furry Kind; 17B, © Anton Zabielskyi/Shutterstock; 18T, © David Dalton/FLPA/Minden Pictures; 18BL, © Sally Anne Thompson/Animal-Photography; 18BR, © Jerry Shulman/SuperStock; 19, © AP Photo/Elliott Minor; 20L, © Nikolai Tsvetkov/Shutterstock; 20TR, © Juniors Bildarchiv/Alamy; 20BR, © Nataliya Kuznetsova/ Shutterstock; 21L, © Vendla Stockdale/Shutterstock; 21R, © Anna Utekhina/Dreamstime; 22, © Sheldon Levis/ Alamy; 23, © Mark Raycroft/Minden Pictures; 24, © Ian Francis/Alamy; 25T, © NHPA/SuperStock; 25B, © Steve Bull/Sirius Photography; 26L, © Scott Mc Kiernan/ZUMA Press/Newscom; 26R, © O.Digoit/Alamy; 27, © Katarzyna Mazurowska/Shutterstock; 28, © Animals Animals/SuperStock; 29T, © Eric Isselée/Shutterstock; 29B, © Sally Anne Thompson/Animal-Photography; 31, © Nikolai Tsvetkov/Shutterstock; 32, © Alexia Khruscheva/Shutterstock.

Publisher: Kenn Goin
Editorial Director: Adam Siegel
Creative Director: Spencer Brinker
Design: Dawn Beard Creative
Cover Design: Dawn Beard Creative and Kim Jones
Photo Researcher: Mary Fran Loftus

Library of Congress Cataloging-in-Publication Data

Lunis, Natalie.
  German shepherd : super smart / by Natalie Lunis.
     p. cm. — (Big dogs rule)
  Includes bibliographical references and index.
  ISBN-13: 978-1-61772-299-8 (library binding)
  ISBN-10: 1-61772-299-5 (library binding)
  1. German shepherd dog—Juvenile literature. I. Title.
  SF429.G37L86 2012
  636.737'6—dc22

                              2011011348

For more information, write to Bearport Publishing Company, Inc., 45 West 21st Street, Suite 3B, New York, New York 10010. Printed in the United States of America in North Mankato, Minnesota.

071511
042711CGD

10 9 8 7 6 5 4 3 2 1

Contents

"Get Help!"

On the evening of April 4, 2010, 23-year-old Ben Heinrichs was working in a garage in his family's yard in Caswell Lakes, Alaska. His dog, a five-year-old German shepherd named Buddy, was keeping him company. All of a sudden, a heater in the small building started a fire.

Ben Heinrichs and his good friend Buddy

Ben received some **minor** burns on his face when the fire flared up. To stay safe, he ran out of the garage right away and closed the door to keep the flames inside. Then he remembered Buddy. He ran back and let the big dog out. Once they were both outside, he told the German shepherd, "We need to get help."

The neighborhood where Ben and his family lived was very **rural**. The houses were far apart from one another, and there was no town nearby.

▲ **Like this cabin that caught on fire, the garage that Ben was working in was not near people or other buildings— so it was not easy to get help quickly.**

5

To the Rescue

Buddy disappeared into the woods. Ben thought that he must have gone somewhere to hide. Instead, however, the dog had run off to look for help—just as his owner had asked him to. After a while, Buddy ran onto a dark country road and spotted just the right person—Alaska **state trooper** Terrence Shanigan.

Buddy and Trooper Shanigan

Trooper Shanigan had been sent to the scene of the fire, after a neighbor called about seeing a burst of flames. The police officer's **GPS** had stopped working, however, so he couldn't find the burning building. Luckily, Buddy found him and took over.

By running ahead of the police car, Buddy guided the trooper to the right place. Once there, the trooper was able to contact firefighters. They arrived just in time to stop the flames from spreading farther and burning down Ben's house.

Buddy was honored as a hero by the Alaska State Police. As a reward for his actions, he received a stainless-steel dog bowl with his name and a message of thanks printed on it.

◄ **Buddy after the rescue**

Hero Hall of Fame

Buddy's story appeared in many newspapers and on television shows. However, he is far from the first German shepherd to win fame for being intelligent, **courageous**, and loyal. For example, almost 100 years ago, another German shepherd—a female also named Buddy— became America's first **guide dog**. She was paired up with a young blind man named Morris Frank. The two of them traveled around the United States to show how guide dogs can safely lead blind people through towns and cities.

Morris Frank, shown here with Buddy, worked to start The Seeing Eye, the first school for guide dogs in the United States. The school, located in Morristown, New Jersey, still trains dogs today.

Guide dogs are trained to know when to stop at street corners and when it is safe to cross. They also know when to disobey their owners' commands in order to keep them safe.

Since then, many German shepherds have worked as guide dogs, police dogs, **search-and-rescue dogs**, and **military dogs**. In events ranging from World War I (1914–1918) to the World Trade Center attack in 2001 to the 2010 earthquake in Haiti, the dogs have bravely served alongside their human **handlers**.

Many specially trained ▶ search-and-rescue dogs, including this German shepherd named Trakr, searched the World Trade Center site for victims. On September 12, 2001, Trakr found the last survivor of the disaster.

◀ Because of their excellent sense of smell, German shepherds are often trained by the police and the military to work as drug-sniffing dogs and bomb-sniffing dogs.

Beginning the Breed

German shepherds were not always raised to be guide dogs or police dogs. Instead—as their name suggests—they were at first **bred** and trained to **herd** sheep. A man named Max von Stephanitz (stuh-FON-its) gave the **breed** its start in Germany during the late 1800s. His goal was to raise the best possible herding dogs.

German shepherds were first bred in Germany, a country in Europe.

In addition to making sure that sheep went or stayed where they were supposed to, German shepherd dogs protected sheep from wolves and other **predators**. They also guarded the **flock** from human thieves.

▲ Today, German shepherds still herd sheep on farms in many parts of the world. The dogs keep all the sheep in a flock together and make sure that they don't eat valuable crops.

Von Stephanitz knew that a good herding dog needed to be intelligent, hardworking, and able to be on the move all day. It also needed to be strong, brave, and loyal to its human owner. One day, at a dog show, von Stephanitz saw a dog that seemed just right. He bought the dog and named him Horand. He started keeping records to keep track of Horand's puppies and the puppies that they ended up having. These dogs, which had **inherited** Horand's intelligence and hardworking nature, became the first German shepherds.

Horand and Max von Stephanitz

Two World Wars

During the early 1900s, people who lived outside of Germany started learning about German shepherds and bringing them to their own countries. Then World War I (1914–1918) broke out. In some ways, it made people admire the dogs even more. Soldiers from countries such as the United States, Great Britain, and France who were fighting in Germany brought home stories about the intelligence and courage of German shepherds that had been trained for war. In other ways, the war hurt the dogs' popularity, since Germany was an enemy to the people who lived in these countries.

Before World War I, people in Germany trained German shepherds to work as police and military dogs. Once the war began, the German army used the dogs to guard prisoners, protect troops, and, as shown here, to deliver messages.

Still, the breed's popularity increased until World War II (1939–1945), when once again Germany was at war with many other countries. As the years went on, however, people outside of Germany started wanting to own German shepherds again—both as working dogs and as pets.

At the end of World War I, an ▶ American soldier in Europe brought home a German shepherd that he had named Rin Tin Tin. The dog went on to star in a series of movies, and his popularity made many people want German shepherds as pets.

◀ During World War II, the United States and other countries fighting Germany also used German shepherds. This dog, for example, served alongside American troops.

World War I and World War II were both worldwide conflicts in which many countries, including Great Britain, France, Russia, and the United States, fought against a group of countries led by Germany.

Size and Shape

Before Max von Stephanitz started breeding German shepherds in the late 1800s, many dogs in his part of Europe were used to herd sheep. However, they looked very different from one another. For example, their bodies were not all the same size and shape.

Because of its wolf-like looks, the German shepherd was once known as the "wolf dog" in England. After a short time, however, it went back to being called a shepherd.

German shepherd

gray wolf

Since the time when von Stephanitz began raising German shepherds, the dogs have become an **official** breed. They have also become much more alike in appearance. German shepherds have wolf-like heads, with wedge-shaped **muzzles** and pointed ears. They are large compared to most other dog breeds. Today, a German shepherd usually stands about 25 inches (64 cm) high at the shoulder. It weighs between 62 and 80 pounds (28 and 36 kg).

A German shepherd is much ▶ larger than a Chihuahua.

▲ **A German shepherd's size and strength are a great help during search-and-rescue work. The dogs are trained to climb ladders to look for injured people and also to drag them to safety.**

Coats and Colors

When most people picture a German shepherd, they see a large dog with a black and tan **coat**. Its hair is neither extra short, like a Dalmatian's, nor long and silky, like an Irish setter's.

A black and tan German shepherd

Surprisingly, this description fits many German shepherds, but it does not match all of them. In addition to black and tan, the dogs can be many other colors, including black and red, black and cream, all black, or all white. Their coats are not always medium-length, either. Some German shepherds have long, silky hair, and some even have long coats that are rough and wiry.

◄ A long-haired black and red German shepherd

A long-haired ► black German shepherd

A white German shepherd

Unlike dark-colored German shepherds, white German shepherds are not usually used as guard dogs because they can be seen too easily at night. However, they still make excellent and lovable pets.

How Smart?

Since the earliest days of the breed, German shepherds have used and shown their intelligence. While herding sheep, they needed to keep an eye on every member of the herd while also watching for outside threats. If a problem arose, the dog would need to figure out what to do and then quickly take action.

A German shepherd herding sheep

▼ **Which dogs rank higher than German shepherds in intelligence? According to the scientists who designed the tests, the border collie is number one. The poodle is number two.**

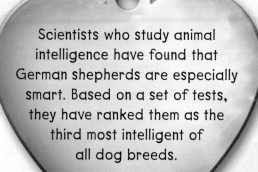
Scientists who study animal intelligence have found that German shepherds are especially smart. Based on a set of tests, they have ranked them as the third most intelligent of all dog breeds.

border collie

poodle

Today, the big dogs continue to show their ability to take charge of a situation. For example, in 2007, Shannon Lorio was thrown from her car when it went off the road and down a steep hill. A German shepherd that had gotten out of his yard found her and dragged her back up to the road. Then he waited with her until someone stopped to help.

▲ After saving Shannon (shown above) in Thomasville, Georgia, this German shepherd was adopted by a dog trainer who wanted to try him out for search-and-rescue work. As part of his new life, the dog was given a new name: Hero.

A Great Pet

German shepherds have not just made it to the top when it comes to intelligence. Year after year, they have also been among the three most popular dog breeds. That's because the same qualities that make the German shepherd a great working dog also make it a great pet.

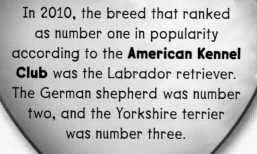

In 2010, the breed that ranked as number one in popularity according to the **American Kennel Club** was the Labrador retriever. The German shepherd was number two, and the Yorkshire terrier was number three.

#1: Labrador retriever

#2: German shepherd

#3: Yorkshire terrier

A German shepherd's intelligence and physical skills, for example, make it a playmate that is full of fun and energy. Its guarding skills make it a great watchdog and protector. Most important of all, its loyalty makes it a faithful friend for life. In fact, many German shepherd owners think of their dogs as furry, four-legged family members.

German shepherds are not just ▶ working dogs. They love to play, too.

German shepherds are known for bonding, or feeling close to, their owners. At the same time, they are often wary, or suspicious, of strangers.

Puppy or Adult?

Many people who decide on a German shepherd as a pet choose to get a puppy. However, puppies are not ready to be taken home as pets until they are about eight weeks old. Before that time, they are tiny and helpless. Rather than eating solid food, they mostly depend on milk from their mother.

There are usually about six puppies in a German shepherd **litter**. The puppies weigh about one pound (.45 kg) when they are born.

Some German shepherd owners start out with older dogs. These dogs usually come from **animal shelters** or **rescue groups**. The people who take care of the dogs in these settings get to know the **personality** of each one well. As a result, they are able to match adult dogs to the right person or family.

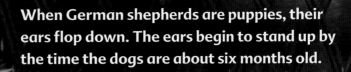
When German shepherds are puppies, their ears flop down. The ears begin to stand up by the time the dogs are about six months old.

Basic Training

Even though pet German shepherds don't have jobs, like police dogs or guide dogs do, they still need plenty of training. If these big, smart dogs don't have something to keep their minds busy, they will become bored and start looking for ways to get into trouble.

Some people think that German shepherds are fierce and unfriendly dogs. However, the dogs usually behave in these ways because they have not been trained to get along with people other than their owners.

Owners should start training their puppies as soon as they are brought home. In addition to **house-training**—learning when and where to go to the bathroom—they need to work on **obedience training**, learning commands such as "sit," "stay," and "down." Just as important, the growing dogs need to be **socialized**. That is, they need to learn how to get along with people and pets who are not part of their own "family."

Once a German shepherd has learned the basic commands, an owner can work with it on more advanced activities, such as **agility trials** or **flyball competitions**. The smart, powerful dogs enjoy the challenges that these events offer.

▲ In an agility competition, dogs race through an obstacle course.

◀ A flyball competition is also an obstacle course. As part of the fun, the dogs catch a tennis ball.

A Big Responsibility

Owning any kind of dog is a big responsibility, but owning a big dog such as a German shepherd is an even bigger responsibility. Like any other dog, a German shepherd needs the right food, exercise, **grooming**, and check-ups from a **veterinarian**. However, a dog of this breed also has its own special needs. For example, German shepherds are **athletic**, so they need more exercise than many other breeds—about two walks each day and time for play where they can catch or chase balls.

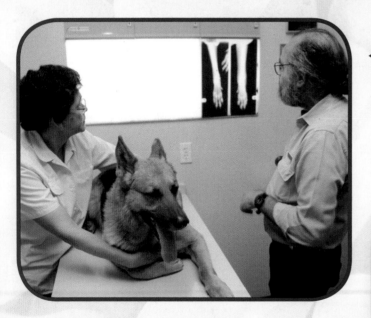

◀ Like other breeds of large dogs, German shepherds may have problems with their hip or elbow bones. Veterinarians can check for these problems.

German shepherds shed a ▶ lot of hair during the fall and spring. At these times, they need to be brushed every day.

Pet owners who want to share their homes with one of these big dogs need to learn all about them. After all, German shepherds are eager to work hard and eager to please the people in their lives. As a result, they deserve caring owners who are willing to give the loyal and loving dogs everything that they need.

Even though most people simply say "German shepherd," the official name of the breed is *German shepherd dog.*

Some dogs can spend a lot of time on their own—but not German shepherds. They like to keep their families in sight—and know that they are safe and sound.

German Shepherds at a Glance

Weight:	62–80 pounds (28–36 kg)
Height at Shoulder:	22–26 inches (56–66 cm)
Coat Hair:	Medium-length or long; smooth and straight or slightly rough and wiry
Colors:	Usually black and tan, though the coat may be other colors, including black and cream, black and red, all black, all white, or blue, which is actually a bluish-gray
Country of Origin:	Germany
Life Span:	11–13 years
Personality:	Brave, loyal, and intelligent; eager to please its owners; sometimes suspicious of strangers

Best in Show

What makes a great German shepherd? Every owner knows that his or her dog is special. Judges in dog shows, however, look very carefully at a German shepherd's appearance and behavior. Here are some of the things they look for:

head is strong-looking with a wedge-shaped muzzle

ears are large and pointed, especially when at attention

Behavior: alert, confident, and hardworking

eyes are dark, medium-size, and almond-shaped with an intelligent expression

back legs should be strong and muscular

neck is strong and muscular

chest should be wide and strong-looking

front legs should be straight and muscular

tail is bushy and slightly curved

Glossary

agility trials (uh-JIL-uh-tee TRYE-uhlz) contests in which dogs go through a course set up with jumps, objects to climb, and other special features

American Kennel Club (uh-MER-i-kuhn KEN-uhl KLUHB) a national organization that is involved in many activities having to do with dogs, including collecting information about dog breeds and setting rules for dog shows

animal shelters (AN-uh-muhl SHEL-turz) places where homeless pets are taken care of while waiting for new places to live

athletic (ath-LET-ik) active

bred (BRED) raised

breed (BREED) a kind of dog

coat (KOHT) the fur on dogs or other animals

courageous (kuh-RAY-juhss) brave

flock (FLOK) a group of one kind of animal, such as sheep, goats, or birds

flyball competitions (FLYE-bawl kom-puh-TISH-uhnz) contests in which dogs run, jump, and catch tennis balls

GPS (jee-pee-ESS) letters standing for Global Positioning System; a space-based navigation satellite system that provides accurate location information

grooming (GROOM-ing) keeping an animal neat and clean

guide dog (GIDE DAWG) a dog that is trained to lead blind people

handlers (HAND-lurz) people who train and work with dogs or other animals

herd (HURD) to lead individuals into a group

house-training (HAUS-trayn-ing) learning to go to the bathroom outdoors

inherited (in-HER-uh-tid) received traits from a parent

litter (LIT-ur) a group of baby animals that are born to the same mother at the same time

military dogs (MIL-uh-ter-ee DAWGZ) dogs that work with members of the armed forces

minor (MYE-nur) small, not important

muzzles (MUHZ-uhlz) the mouth, nose, and jaw areas of dogs

obedience training (oh-BEE-dee-uhnss TRAYN-ing) learning to follow commands such as "sit" and "stay"

official (uh-FISH-uhl) approved by people who are in charge

personality (pur-suh-NAL-uh-tee) the special habits and ways of behaving that make an animal different from others

predators (PRED-uh-turz) animals that hunt and eat other animals

rescue groups (RES-kyoo GROOPS) groups of people who work together to find homes for homeless pets

rural (RUR-uhl) country-like, not city-like

search-and-rescue dogs (SURCH-AND-RES-kyoo DAWGZ) dogs that look for survivors after a disaster, such as an earthquake

socialized (SOH-shuhl-eyezd) taught to get along with people or other animals

state trooper (STAYT TROO-pur) a state police officer

veterinarian (vet-ur-uh-NER-ee-uhn) a doctor who takes care of dogs and other animals

Bibliography

Coile, D. Caroline. *German Shepherds for Dummies.* New York: Hungry Minds (2000).

Kern, Francis G. *German Shepherds.* Neptune City, NJ: T.F.H. Publications (2003).

Rice, Dan. *Big Dog Breeds.* Hauppauge, NY: Barron's (2001).

Victor, Cindy. *German Shepherd Dog.* Neptune City, NJ: T.F.H. Publications (2010).

Read More

Gray, Susan H. *German Shepherds (Domestic Dogs).* Mankato, MN: Child's World (2008).

Ingebretsen, Karen. *German Shepherds and Other Herding Dogs.* Chicago: World Book (2010).

Schuh, Mari. *German Shepherds (Dog Breeds).* Minneapolis, MN: Bellwether Media (2009).

Learn More Online

To learn more about German shepherds, visit
www.bearportpublishing.com/BigDogsRule

Index

About the Author

Natalie Lunis has written many nonfiction books for children. She lives in the Hudson River Valley, just north of New York City.